Hey Caroline,

So now you're 5 years old and such a Little ~~Princess~~.

Although you're on the quiet side, you know exactly what you want and will settle for nothing less (and thats a good thing).

Caroline, remember. Granddaughters are like Birthday Cake, Sweet and Pretty, and the best thing in the house!!!

Love & Prayers
Mamaw Taylor

9/07

# What Little Girls Do...

99 00 01 02 03 RDS 10 9 8 7 6 5 4 3 2 1

www.andrewsmcmeel.com

Library of Congress Cataloging-in-Publication Data
Hickerson, Robert.
    What little girls do-- / Robert Hickerson.
      p.  cm.
    ISBN 0-7407-0093-6 (hc.)
    1. Girls Portraits. 2. Portrait photography. I. Title.
TR681.G5H53  1999
779'.25'092--dc21

99-21529
CIP

Design by Holly Camerlinck

─── ATTENTION: SCHOOLS AND BUSINESSES ───

Andrews McMeel books are available at quantity discounts with bulk purchase for educational, business, or sales promotional use. For information, please write to: Special Sales Department, Andrews McMeel Publishing, 4520 Main Street, Kansas City, Missouri 64111.

# What Little Girls Do...

Robert Hickerson

**Andrews McMeel
Publishing**

Kansas City

Glow

Mimie

Snuggle

Go for it

Create

# Compete

*Pamper*

Giggle

# Huddle

Quench

# Charm

# Practice, practice, practice, practice

# See things
## my way

Share

Swoosh

Giddy-up

*Nurture*

See
**eyetoeye**

Reign

*Entertain*

Splash

*Day dream*

Question

# Feast

Primp

Imagine

Nourish

*Search*

## Acknowledgments

I am so fortunate to have a project like this come my way. For that I must thank my dear friend and editor, Jean Zevnik, who pushed me to do my best work, and whose guidance and encouragement help make this a wonderful experience (even when we disagreed). I am grateful to have worked with children who constantly reminded me how to love life. And to all the parents who let me into their child's world, you are the lucky ones to have such great kids whose happiness, honesty, and innocence are beautiful examples for us all to follow.